WRIGHT FAMILY LAND TAX LISTS

1782–1850

ROCKBRIDGE COUNTY VIRGINIA

Robert N. Grant

HERITAGE BOOKS
2010

HERITAGE BOOKS
AN IMPRINT OF HERITAGE BOOKS, INC.

Books, CDs, and more—Worldwide

For our listing of thousands of titles see our website
at
www.HeritageBooks.com

Published 2010 by
HERITAGE BOOKS, INC.
Publishing Division
100 Railroad Ave. #104
Westminster, Maryland 21157

Copyright © 2010 Robert N. Grant

All rights reserved. No part of this book may be reproduced or transmitted in any form or by any means, electronic or mechanical, including photocopying, recording or by any information storage and retrieval system without written permission from the author, except for the inclusion of brief quotations in a review.

International Standard Book Numbers
Paperbound: 978-0-7884-5153-9
Clothbound: 978-0-7884-8322-6

Introduction To Appendices: Land Tax Records, Rockbridge County, Virginia

This document is an appendix to a larger work titled Sorting Some Of The Wrights Of Southern Virginia. The work is divided into parts for each family of Wrights that has been researched. Each part is divided into two sections; the first section is text discussing the family and the evidence supporting the relationships and the second section is a descendants chart summarizing the relationships and information known about each individual.

The appendices to the work (of which this document is one) present source records for persons named Wright by county and by type of record with the identification of the person named and their Wright ancestors to the extent known.

The source for the records listed in this appendix is the following:

    1)   Rockbridge County, Virginia, Land Tax Lists, available from The Library of Virginia, 11th at Capitol, Richmond, Virginia 23219.

The identification of a person or their ancestor by year and county indicates their year of death and county of residence at death. For example, "1763 Thomas Wright of Bedford County" indicates that this was the Thomas Wright who died in 1763 in Bedford County. If no state is listed after the county, the state is Virginia; counties in states other than Virginia will have a state listed after the county, as in "1876 William S. Wright of Highland County, Ohio".

A parenthetical after the name indicates an identification of the person when a place of death is not yet known, as in "John Wright (Goochland County Carpenter)". A county in parentheses after the name indicates the county with which that person was most identified when no evidence of the place of death has yet been found, as in "Grief Wright (Bedford County)".

All or portions of the text and descendants charts for each Wright family identified are available from the author:

    Robert N. Grant
    15 Campo Bello Court   (H) 650-854-0895
    Menlo Park, California 94025   (O) 650-614-3800

This is a work in process and I would be most interested in receiving additional information about any of the persons identified in these records in order to correct any errors or expand on the information given.

1782 THROUGH 1792 LAND TAX LIST

ROCKBRIDGE COUNTY, VIRGINIA

Appendix: Rockbridge County, Virginia, 1782 thru 1792 Land Tax List:

[No Wrights listed]

1793 LAND TAX LIST

ROCKBRIDGE COUNTY, VIRGINIA

Appendix: Rockbridge County, Virginia, 1793 Land Tax List:

						Identification
Charles Wright Trd from Thos Logan		50		7.10	2.3	

1794 THROUGH 1815 LAND TAX LIST

ROCKBRIDGE COUNTY, VIRGINIA

Appendix: Rockbridge County, Virginia, 1794 thru 1815 Land Tax List:

[No Wrights listed]

1816 LAND TAX LIST

ROCKBRIDGE COUNTY, VIRGINIA

Appendix: Rockbridge County, Virginia, 1816 Land Tax List:

List A:

Name of Owner	Residence	Estate	No of Town Lotts	Name of the Town	Yearly Rent of Lotts $ Cts	Amt of Taxes upon Lotts at in $ Cts	Number of acres of land	Description	Identification

[No Wrights listed]

Appendix: Rockbridge County, Virginia, 1816 Land Tax List:

List B:

Names of Owners	Residence	Estate	No of Town Lots	Name of the Town	Yearly rent of Lots $ Cts	Amt of Taxes upon Lots at ____ in $ Cts	Number of acres of Land	General Description	Distance & bearing from the Ct house	Rate of Land per Acre
Robert Wright	Rockbg.	fee Simple	31	Fairfield	6.00	.18			13 NE	

Appendix: Rockbridge County, Virginia, 1816 Land Tax List:

List B:

Names of Owners [continued from prior page]	Total value of Land $ Cts	Amot of tax upon Land at __ per $ Cts	Total of tax on Lots & Land $ Cts	Explanation of Alterations during the preceding year	Identification
Robert Wright			.18	Trd. from Tho. Simpson by Sale	1847 Robert Wright of Rockbridge County

1817 THROUGH 1833 LAND TAX LIST

ROCKBRIDGE COUNTY, VIRGINIA

Appendix: Rockbridge County, Virginia, 1817 thru 1833 Land Tax List:

[No Wrights listed]

1834 LAND TAX LIST

ROCKBRIDGE COUNTY, VIRGINIA

Appendix: Rockbridge County, Virginia, 1834 Land Tax List:

List A:

Name of Owner	Residence	Estate	No of acres Land	Description of the Land	Identification

[No Wrights listed]

Appendix: Rockbridge County, Virginia, 1834 Land Tax List:

List B:

	Residence	Estate	Acres of land		distc. & bearing	Land p A includ. Buildgs	Added to the land on a/c of Buildgs	Total Value
John Wright	Rockbr	fee	16¼	on Little C P river adj Jos: Bell &c	18N	2.50		40.00

Appendix: Rockbridge County, Virginia, 1834 Land Tax List:

List B:

[continued from prior page]	Amot of tax @ 8 cts per	Explanation of Alterations	Identification
John Wright	.04	Transfd from Jas. Elliot	1836 John Wright of Rockbridge County

1835 LAND TAX LIST

ROCKBRIDGE COUNTY, VIRGINIA

Appendix: Rockbridge County, Virginia, 1835 Land Tax List:

List A:

Name of Owner	Residence	Estate	Number of acres Land	Description of the land	Identification

[No Wrights listed]

Appendix: Rockbridge County, Virginia, 1835 Land Tax List:

List B:

Owners Names	Residn.	estate	qty of land	description of the land	distc. & bearing	Land p A includ. Buildgs	Added to Ld. on a/c of Buildgs	Total Value
John Wright	Rockbr	fee	16¼	on Little C P river adj Jos: Bell &c	18N	2.50		40.00

Appendix: Rockbridge County, Virginia, 1835 Land Tax List:

List B:

Owners Names [continued from prior page]	Amot of tax at 8 cts per	Explanation of Alterations	Identification
John Wright	.04		1836 John Wright of Rockbridge County

1836 LAND TAX LIST

ROCKBRIDGE COUNTY, VIRGINIA

Appendix: Rockbridge County, Virginia, 1836 Land Tax List:

List A:

Name of Owner	Residence	Estate	No of acres Land	Distance & bearing from the C. House	Description of the land	Distn & bearg	Ld. p a includ. Buildgs	Added to Ld. on a/c of Buildgs	Total Value

[No Wrights listed]

Appendix: Rockbridge County, Virginia, 1836 Land Tax List:

List A:

| Name of Owner [continued from prior page] | Amot of tax | Explanation of alterations | Identification |

[No Wrights listed]

Appendix: Rockbridge County, Virginia, 1836 Land Tax List:

List B:

Owners of Land	residence	Estate	Acres of land	Description of the land	Distn & bearg	Ld. p a includ. Buildgs	Added to Ld. on a/c of Buildgs	Total Value
John Wright	Rockbr	fee	16¼	on Little C P R adj Joseph Bell	18N	2.50		40.00

Appendix: Rockbridge County, Virginia, 1836 Land Tax List:

List B:

Owners of Land [continued from prior page]	Amot of tax	Explanation of alterations	Identification
John Wright	.04		1836 John Wright of Rockbridge County

26.

1837 LAND TAX LIST

ROCKBRIDGE COUNTY, VIRGINIA

Appendix: Rockbridge County, Virginia, 1837 Land Tax List:

List A:

Name of Owner	residce	Estate	Acres of Land	Description of the land	distn & bearg	Land p a includ. buildgs	Added to Land on a/c of buildgs	Total Value	Amot of tax	Explanation of alterations	Identification

[No Wrights listed]

Appendix: Rockbridge County, Virginia, 1837 Land Tax List:

List B:

Owners of Land	residce	Estate	Acres of land	description of the land	distn & bearg	Land p a includ. buildgs	Added to Land on a/c of buildgs	Total Value
John Wright (Heirs	Rockbr	fee	16¼	on Little C P R adj Jos. Bell	18N	2.50		40.00

Appendix: Rockbridge County, Virginia, 1837 Land Tax List:

List B:

Owners of Land [continued from prior page]	Amot of tax	Explanation of alterations	Identification
John Wright (Heirs	.04		1836 John Wright of Rockbridge County

1838 LAND TAX LIST

ROCKBRIDGE COUNTY, VIRGINIA

Appendix: Rockbridge County, Virginia, 1838 Land Tax List:

List A:

_____ _____ ___ _____ _____ _____
                                              Identification

[No Wrights listed]

Appendix: Rockbridge County, Virginia, 1838 Land Tax List:

List B:

Owners of Land	Residn	Estate	Acres of Ld.	Description of the land	distn & bearg	Land p a includ. buildgs	Added to the ld. on a/c of buildgs	Total Value
John Wright (Heirs) Do Little poss			16¼	on the Nob adj: Jos: Bell Wats Big C.P.R.	18N	2.50		40.00

Appendix: Rockbridge County, Virginia, 1838 Land Tax List:

List B:

Owners of Land [continued from prior page]	Amot of tax 10¢ pr	Explanation of alterations	Identification
John Wright (Heirs) Do Little poss	.04		1836 John Wright of Rockbridge County

Appendix: Rockbridge County, Virginia, 1838 Land Tax List:

List C:

Owners	Residn	Estate	No of Town Lots	Name of Town	Value of Buildgs	Value of lots includ. buildgs	Yearly rent of lots	Amt of tax	Explanation of alterations	Identification
Robert Wright	Rockbr	fee	1 35	F F	.60	.75	15.00	.38		1847 Robert Wright of Rockbridge County

36.

1839 LAND TAX LIST

ROCKBRIDGE COUNTY, VIRGINIA

Appendix: Rockbridge County, Virginia, 1839 Land Tax List:

List A:

Name of owner	Residence	Estate	No of acres Land	Description of the Land Adjoining whom	Identification
[No Wrights listed]					

Appendix: Rockbridge County, Virginia, 1839 Land Tax List:

List B:

Names of Owners	residn	Estate	Acres of ld.	description of the land	distn & bearg	Ld. p a includ. buildgs	Added to Ld. on a/c of buildgs	Total Value
John Wright Heirs			16¼	on the Nob adj: Jos: Bell Wats Big CPR	18N	2.50		40.00

Appendix: Rockbridge County, Virginia, 1839 Land Tax List:

List B:

Names of Owners [continued from prior page]	amot of tax 10¢ pr	Explanation of Alterations	Identification
John Wright Heirs	.04		1836 John Wright of Rockbridge County

Appendix: Rockbridge County, Virginia, 1839 Land Tax List:

List C:

Owners Names	residn	Estate	No of town lots	Name of Town	Value of Buildgs	Value of lots includ. buildgs	Yearly rent of lots @ 2.50	Amot of tax	Explanation of alterations	Identification
Robert Wright	Rockbr	fee	1 35	F F	.60	.75	15.00	.38		1847 Robert Wright of Rockbridge County

1840 LAND TAX LIST

ROCKBRIDGE COUNTY, VIRGINIA

Appendix: Rockbridge County, Virginia, 1840 Land Tax List:

List A:

_____ _____ ___ _____ _____ _____

[No Wrights listed]

_____
Identification

Appendix: Rockbridge County, Virginia, 1840 Land Tax List:

List B:

Names of Owners	Residn	Kind of Estate	Number of Acres of land	Description of the land	distn & bearg from C Ho.	Value of ___ includ. buildgs	Sum added to the Value of the land on a/c of buildgs	Total Value
Thompson A. Wright	Rockg	fee	58.120	adj Martha Johnston	8 NE	3.50		205.62
John Wright Heirs poss Jos: Bell	Rockg	poss	16.40	adj Joseph Bell on the Nob wats BCPR	18 N	2.00		32.50

Appendix: Rockbridge County, Virginia, 1840 Land Tax List:

List B:

Names of Owners [continued from prior page]	amot of tax 10¢ pr	Remarks	Identification
Thompson A Wright	.21	transfd from Jas West	1854 Thompson A. Wright of Rockbridge County, son of 1815 John Wright of Prince William County, grandson of William Wright, great grandson of 1765 Richard Wright of Prince William County, and possibly great great grandson of 1700 Richard Wright of Stafford County
John Wright Heirs poss Jos: Bell	.04		1836 John Wright of Rockbridge County

Appendix: Rockbridge County, Virginia, 1840 Land Tax List:

List C:

Names of Owners	residence	Kind of Estate	Number of town lots	Name of town	description of town lots	Value of lots includ. buildgs	Sum added to value of lots on a/c of buildgs	Yearly rent of lots
Robert Wright	Rockbr	fee		F F	1 on NW side of Mn Stt	.75	60.00	15.00

Appendix: Rockbridge County, Virginia, 1840 Land Tax List:

List C:

Names of Owners [continued from prior page]	amot of tax	Remarks	Identification
Robert Wright	.38		1847 Robert Wright of Rockbridge County

1841 LAND TAX LIST

ROCKBRIDGE COUNTY, VIRGINIA

Appendix: Rockbridge County, Virginia, 1841 Land Tax List:

List A:

Name of Owner	Residence	Kind of Estate	No of acres	Description of the land	Distn & bearg from the ct house	Value of the land pr acre	Value of the buildings	Value of the land and buildings	Identification

[No Wrights listed]

Appendix: Rockbridge County, Virginia, 1841 Land Tax List:

List B:

Name of Owner	Residn	Estate	Acres of land	description of the Land	distn & bearg from Co Ho.	Value of __ includ. buildgs	Sum added to Value of L on a/c of buildgs	Total Value
Thompson A. Wright	Rockbr	fee	58.120	adj Martha Johnston	8 NE	3.50		205.62
John Wright Heirs Jos: Bell poss	Rockbr	fee	16.40	adj J Bell on Nob Wats Big C.P.R.	18 N	2.00		32.50

2631(070609)

Appendix: Rockbridge County, Virginia, 1841 Land Tax List:

List B:

Names of Owners [continued from prior page]	amot of tax @ 12½¢	Explanation	Identification
Thompson A Wright	.26		1854 Thompson A. Wright of Rockbridge County, son of 1815 John Wright of Prince William County, grandson of William Wright, great grandson of 1765 Richard Wright of Prince William County, and possibly great great grandson of 1700 Richard Wright of Stafford County
John Wright Heirs Jos: Bell poss	.05		1836 John Wright of Rockbridge County

Appendix: Rockbridge County, Virginia, 1841 Land Tax List:

List C:

Name of Owner	Residence	Estate	Number of __ lots in town	Name of town	Value of buildgs	Value of lots including Buildg	Yearly rent of lots	Amot of tax on lots @ $3 per	Explanation of alterations	Identification
Robert Wright	Rockbr	fee	1	F F	60.00	75.00	15.00	.45		1847 Robert Wright of Rockbridge County

54.

1842 LAND TAX LIST

ROCKBRIDGE COUNTY, VIRGINIA

Appendix: Rockbridge County, Virginia, 1842 Land Tax List:

List A:

Names of Owners	residn	Estate	Acres of land	Description of the Land	distn & bearg from C H	Land p a includg buildgs	added to the land on a/c of buildgs	Total Value
Thompson A. Wright	Rockbg	fee	58.120	adj Martha Johnston	8 NE	3.50		205.62
John Wright hs Joseph Bell possn	Rockbr	unkn	16.40	adj Joseph Bell on Nob Wats Big C.P.R	18 N	2.00		32.50

2631(070609)

Appendix: Rockbridge County, Virginia, 1842 Land Tax List:

List A:

Names of Owners [continued from prior page]	Tax @ 12½¢	Explanation	Identification
Thompson A Wright	.26		1854 Thompson A. Wright of Rockbridge County, son of 1815 John Wright of Prince William County, grandson of William Wright, great grandson of 1765 Richard Wright of Prince William County, and possibly great great grandson of 1700 Richard Wright of Stafford County
John Wright hs Joseph Bell possn	.05		1836 John Wright of Rockbridge County

Appendix: Rockbridge County, Virginia, 1842 Land Tax List:

List B:

Name of Owner	Residn.	Estate	No of each lot in the town	Name of Town	Value of Buildgs	Value of lots including buildgs	Yearly rent of lots	Tax on lots at $3 per	Explanations	Identification
Robert Wright	Rockbr	fee	1 lot	Fairfield	60.00	75.00	15.00	.45		1847 Robert Wright of Rockbridge County
William G Wright			1 lot	B B	100.00	150.00	30.00	.90	Transfd from Wm B__	1904 William G. Wright of Rockbridge County, son of 1877 James Wright of August County

2631(070609)

1843 LAND TAX LIST

ROCKBRIDGE COUNTY, VIRGINIA

Appendix: Rockbridge County, Virginia, 1843 Land Tax List:

List A:

Owner of land	Residn	Estate	Acres of land	description	dist & bearing	Ld p a includg buildgs	Added to ld on a/c of buildgs	total Value
Thompson A. Wright			58.120	adj Martha Johnston	7 N	3.50		205.62
Same			100	adj J McKinzie	18 NE	4.00	25.00	400.00
Same			200	adj Manuel Reid	15 NE	7.00	150.00	1400.00
John Wright hs Joseph Bell poss	unkn		16.40	adj Jos: Bell on Nob big C.P.R	18 N	2.00		32.50

Appendix: Rockbridge County, Virginia, 1843 Land Tax List:

List A:

Owner of land [continued from prior page]	Tax at 15 cts per	Explanation	Identification
Thompson A Wright	.31		1854 Thompson A. Wright of Rockbridge County, son of 1815 John Wright of Prince William County, grandson of William Wright, great grandson of 1765 Richard Wright of Prince William County, and possibly great great grandson of 1700 Richard Wright of Stafford County
Same	.60	Trd. from G Wiseman hs	
Same	2.10	Trd. from W Renney	
John Wright hs Joseph Bell poss	.05		1836 John Wright of Rockbridge County

Appendix: Rockbridge County, Virginia, 1843 Land Tax List:

List B:

Names of Owners	Residn.	Estate	No of Each lot in the town	Name of Town	Value of Buildgs	Value of lots inclug buildgs	Yearly rent of lots	Amot Tax $3 60¢ per	Explanations	Identification
Robert Wright	Rockbr	fee	1 lot	F F	60.00	75.00	15.00	.54		1847 Robert Wright of Rockbridge County
William G Wright			1 lot	B B	100.00	150.00	30.00	1.08		1904 William G. Wright of Rockbridge County, son of 1877 James Wright of August County

2631(070609)

1844 LAND TAX LIST

ROCKBRIDGE COUNTY, VIRGINIA

Appendix: Rockbridge County, Virginia, 1844 Land Tax List:

Northern District:

Owner of land	Residence	Estate	Acres of land	Description of the land	distance & Bearing	Value of ld. pr A. Includg Buildings	added on a/c of Buildings	Total Value
Thompson A. Wright			58.120	Martha Johston	7 N	3.50		
Same			100	Jno McKinzie	18 NE	4.00	25.00	
Same Wm Norcross poss			200	Manuel Reid	15 NE	7.00	150.00	
John Wright hs	Unkn		16.40	Jno M Bell on Nobb big C.P River	18 N	2.00		32.50

2631(070609)

Appendix: Rockbridge County, Virginia, 1844 Land Tax List:

Northern District:

Owners of land [continued from prior page]	Tax		Identification
Thompson A Wright Same Same Wm Norcross poss			1854 Thompson A. Wright of Rockbridge County, son 1815 John Wright of Prince William County, grandson of William Wright, great grandson of 1765 Richard Wright of Prince William County, and possibly great great grandson of 1700 Richard Wright of Stafford County
John Wright hs	.06	Jos Bell poss	1836 John Wright of Rockbridge County

Appendix: Rockbridge County, Virginia, 1844 Land Tax List:

Samuel Walkup District:

Owner of land	Residence	Estate	Acres of land	Description of the land	distance & Bearing	Value of ld pr A. Includg Buildings	added on a/c of Buildings	Total Value

No Wrights listed

Appendix: Rockbridge County, Virginia, 1844 Land Tax List:

Samuel Walkup District:

Owners of land
[continued from
prior page]   Tax   Identification

No Wrights listed

Appendix: Rockbridge County, Virginia, 1844 Land Tax List:

List C:

Name of Owner	Residence	Estate	No of Each Lot	Name of Town	value of Buildgs	Value of Lots Including buildings	yearly rent of Lots	tax 2$		Identification
Robert Wright	Rockbr		1		60.00	75.00	15.00	.45		1847 Robert Wright of Rockbridge County
William G Wright			1	B B	100.00	150.00	30.00	.90		1904 William G. Wright of Rockbridge County, son of 1877 James Wright of August County

2631(070609)

1845 LAND TAX LIST

ROCKBRIDGE COUNTY, VIRGINIA

Appendix: Rockbridge County, Virginia, 1845 Land Tax List:

Samuel Walkup District:

Name of Owner	Residence	Estate, whether held in fee simple, for life, &c	No. of Acres	Description of the land, as to watercourses, mountains and contiguous tracts	Distance and bearing from the court-house	Value of land per acre, including buildings	Sum added to the land on account of buildings	Total value of the land and buildings

No Wrights listed

Appendix: Rockbridge County, Virginia, 1845 Land Tax List:

Samuel Walkup District:

Name of Owner [continued from prior page]	Am't of tax on the whole tract, at the legal rate		Identification

No Wrights listed

Appendix: Rockbridge County, Virginia, 1845 Land Tax List:

Samuel Gold District:

Name of Owner	Residence	Estate, whether held in fee simple, for life, &c	No. of Acres	Description of the land, as to watercourses, mountains and continguous tracts	Distance and bearing from the court-house	Value of land per acre, including buildings	Sum added to the land on account of buildings	Total value of the land and buildings
Thompson A. Wright			58.120	Martha Johston	7 N	3.50		205.62
Same			100	His own land	18 NE	4.00	25.00	400.00
Same			200	Maniel Reid	15	7.00	150.00	1600.00
Same			54	Hull & his own land	16	2.50	50.00	135.00
John Wright hs	Unkn		16.40	Jno. Bell on Nobb B.C.P.R.	18 N	2.00		32.50

Appendix: Rockbridge County, Virginia, 1845 Land Tax List:

Samuel Gold District:

Name of Owner [continued from prior page]	Am't of tax on the whole tract, at the legal rate		Identification
Thompson A Wright	.20		1854 Thompson A. Wright of Rockbridge County, son of 1815 John Wright of Prince William County, grandson of William Wright, great grandson of 1765 Richard Wright of Prince William County, and possibly great great grandson of 1700 Richard Wright of Stafford County
Same	.40		
Same	1.40	Wm. Norsop poss	
Same	.13	Transfr Jno McKinsey in 44	
John Wright hs	.03	Jos Bell poss	1836 John Wright of Rockbridge County

2631(070609)

73.

Appendix: Rockbridge County, Virginia, 1845 Land Tax List:

List C:

Name of Owner	Residence	Estate, whether In fee simple, for life, &c	Number of each lot in the the Town	Name of Town	Value of buildings	Value of lots, including buildings	Yearly rent of lots	Amount of tax on lots at the legal rate
Robert Wright	Rockbridge	Fee	1		60.00	75.00	15.00	.36
William G Wright			1	B. Burgh	100.00	150.00	30.00	.72

Appendix: Rockbridge County, Virginia, 1845 Land Tax List:

List C:

Name of Owner [continued from prior page]	Explanation of alterations during the preceding year	Identification
Robert Wright		1847 Robert Wright of Rockbridge County
William G Wright		1904 William G. Wright of Rockbridge County, son of 1877 James Wright of August County

76.

1846 LAND TAX LIST

ROCKBRIDGE COUNTY, VIRGINIA

Appendix: Rockbridge County, Virginia, 1846 Land Tax List:

Samuel Walkup District:

Name of Owner	Residence	Estate, whether held in fee simple, for life, &c	No. of Acres	Description of the land, as to watercourses, mountains and continguous tracts	Distance and bearing from the court house	Value of land per acre, including buildings	Sum added to the land on account of buildings	Total value of the land and buildings

No Wrights listed

Appendix: Rockbridge County, Virginia, 1846 Land Tax List:

Samuel Walkup District:

Name of Owner	Residence	Estate, whether held in fee simple, for life, &c	No. of Acres	Description of the land, as to watercourses, mountains and continguous tracts	Distance and bearing from the courthouse	Value of land per acre, including buildings	Sum added to the land on account of buildings	Total value of the land and buildings

No Wrights listed

Appendix: Rockbridge County, Virginia, 1846 Land Tax List:

Samuel Gold District:

Name of Owner	Residence	Estate, whether held in fee simple, for life, &c	No. of Acres	Description of the land, as to watercourses, mountains and continguous tracts	Distance and bearing from the court-house	Value of land per acre, including buildings	Sum added to the land on account of buildings	Total value of the land and buildings
Thompson A. Wright			58.120	Martha Johston	7 N	3.50		205.62
" " "			100	His own land	18 NE	4.00	25.00	400.00
" " "			200	Emaniel Reid	15	7.00	150.00	1600.00
" " "			54	Jas. Hull & his own land	16	2.50	50.00	135.00
John Wright hs	Unkn		16.40	Jno. M. Bell on Nob B. & L.6 P	18 N	2.00		32.50

Appendix: Rockbridge County, Virginia, 1846 Land Tax List:

Samuel Gold District:

Name of Owner [continued from prior page]	Am't of tax on the whole tract, at the legal rate	Explanation of alterations during the preceding year, especially from whom transferred	Identification
Thompson A Wright	.20		1854 Thompson A. Wright of Rockbridge County, son of 1815 John Wright of Prince William County, grandson of William Wright, great grandson of 1765 Richard Wright of Prince William County, and possibly great great grandson of 1700 Richard Wright of Stafford County
" " "	.40		
" " "	1.40	Wm. Norcross poss	
" " "	.13		
John Wright hs	.03	Jos Bell poss	1836 John Wright of Rockbridge County

Appendix: Rockbridge County, Virginia, 1846 Land Tax List:

List C:

Name of Owner	Residence	Estate	No. of Lot	Name of Town	Value of Buildings	Value of lots Inclng buildings	yearly rent of lots	Amot. of tax
Robert Wright	Rockbige		1		60.00	75.00	15.00	.36
William G Wright			1	Brownsburg	100.00	150.00	30.00	.72

2631(070609)

Appendix: Rockbridge County, Virginia, 1846 Land Tax List:

List C:

Name of Owner [continued from prior page]	Explanation	Identification
Robert Wright		1847 Robert Wright of Rockbridge County
William G Wright		1904 William G. Wright of Rockbridge County, son of 1877 James Wright of August County

1847 LAND TAX LIST

ROCKBRIDGE COUNTY, VIRGINIA

Appendix: Rockbridge County, Virginia, 1847 Land Tax List:

<u>Samuel Walkup District</u>:

Name of Owner	Residence	Estate, whether held In fee simple, for life, &c	No. of Acres	Description of the land, as to watercourses, mountains and continguous tracts	Distance and bear- ing from the court- house	Value of land per acre, including buildings	Sum added to the land on account of buildings	Total value of the land and buildings

No Wrights listed

Appendix: Rockbridge County, Virginia, 1847 Land Tax List:

Samuel Walkup District:

Name of Owner [continued from prior page]	Am't of tax on the whole tract, at the legal rate	Explanation of alterations during the preceding year, especially from whom transferred	Identification

No Wrights listed

Appendix: Rockbridge County, Virginia, 1847 Land Tax List:

<u>Samuel Gold District:</u>

Name of Owner	Residence	Estate, whether held in fee simple, for life, &c	No. of Acres	Description of the land, as to watercourses, mountains and continguous tracts	Distance and bearing from the court-house	Value of land per acre, including buildings	Sum added to the land on account of buildings	Total value of the land and buildings
Thompson A. Wright			58.120	Martha Johston hr	7 N	3.50		205.62
same			100	His own land	18 NE	4.00	25.00	400.00
same			200	Emaniel Reid	15	7.00	150.00	1400.00
same			54	Jas. Hull & his own	16	12.50	50.00	135.00
John Wright hs	Unkn		16.40	Jno. M. Bell on Nobb BBCPR	18 N	2.00		32.50

Appendix: Rockbridge County, Virginia, 1847 Land Tax List:

Samuel Gold District:

Name of Owner [continued from prior page]	Am't of tax on the whole tract, at the legal rate	Explanation of alterations during the preceding year, especially from whom transferred	Identification
Thompson A Wright	.20		1854 Thompson A. Wright of Rockbridge County, son of 1815 John Wright of Prince William County, grandson of William Wright, great grandson of 1765 Richard Wright of Prince William County, and possibly great great grandson of 1700 Richard Wright of Stafford County
same	.40		
same	1.40	Wm. Norcross poss	
same	.13		
John Wright hs	.03	Jos Bell in poss	1836 John Wright of Rockbridge County

2631(070609)

89.

Appendix: Rockbridge County, Virginia, 1847 Land Tax List:

List C:

Name of Owner	Residence	Estate, whether in fee simple, for life, &c	Number of each lot in the Town	Name of Town	Value of buildings	Value of lots, including buildings	Yearly rent of lots	Amount of tax on lots at the legal rate
Robert Wright	Rockbige				60.00	75.00	15.00	.36
William G Wright			1	B. Burg	100.00	150.00	30.00	.72

Appendix: Rockbridge County, Virginia, 1847 Land Tax List:

List C:

Name of Owner [continued from prior page]	Explanation of alterations during the preceding year	Identification
Robert Wright		1847 Robert Wright of Rockbridge County
William G Wright		1904 William G. Wright of Rockbridge County, son of 1877 James Wright of August County

1848 LAND TAX LIST

ROCKBRIDGE COUNTY, VIRGINIA

Appendix: Rockbridge County, Virginia, 1848 Land Tax List:

Samuel Walkup District:

Name of Owner	Residence	Estate, whether held in fee simple, for life, &c	No. of Acres	Description of the land, as to watercourses, mountains and continguous tracts	Distance and bearing from the court-house	Value of land per acre, including buildings	Sum added to the land on account of buildings	Total value of the land and buildings

No Wrights listed

Appendix: Rockbridge County, Virginia, 1848 Land Tax List:

Samuel Walkup District:

Name of Owner [continued from prior page]	Am't of tax on the whole tract, at the legal rate	Explanation of alterations during the preceding year, especially from whom transferred	Identification

No Wrights listed

Appendix: Rockbridge County, Virginia, 1848 Land Tax List:

Samuel Gold District:

Name of Owner	Residence	Estate, whether held in fee simple, for life, &c	No. of Acres	Description of the land, as to watercourses, mountains and continguous tracts	Distance and bearing from the courthouse	Value of land per acre, including buildings	Sum added to the land on account of buildings	Total value of the land and buildings
Thompson A. Wright			58.120	Martha Johston hr	7 N	3.50		205.62
Same			100	His own land	18 NE	4.00	25.00	400.00
Same			200	Emaniel Reid	15	7.00	150.00	1400.00
Same			54	Jas. Hull & his own	16	12.50	50.00	135.00
John Wright hs	unkn		16.40	Jno. M. Bell on Nobb B.C. River	18 N	2.00		32.50

Appendix: Rockbridge County, Virginia, 1848 Land Tax List:

Samuel Gold District:

Name of Owner [continued from prior page]	Am't of tax on the whole tract, at the legal rate	Explanation of alterations during the preceding year, especially from whom transferred	Identification
Thompson A Wright	.20		1854 Thompson A. Wright of Rockbridge County, son of 1815 John Wright of Prince William County, grandson of William Wright, great grandson of 1765 Richard Wright of Prince William County, and possibly great great grandson of 1700 Richard Wright of Stafford County
Same	.40		
Same	1.40	Wm. Norcross	
Same	.13		
John Wright hs	.03	Jos Bell	1836 John Wright of Rockbridge County

Appendix: Rockbridge County, Virginia, 1848 Land Tax List:

List C:

Name of Owner	Residence	Estate	No. of lots	Name of Town	value of Buildings	value of Lots Including Buildings	yearly rent @ $2.50	Amt of tax
Robert Wright	Rockbige		1		60.00	75.00	15.00	.36
William G Wright			1	B Burg	100.00	150.00	30.00	.72

Appendix: Rockbridge County, Virginia, 1848 Land Tax List:

List C:

Name of Owner [continued from prior page]	Identification
Robert Wright	1847 Robert Wright of Rockbridge County
William G Wright	1904 William G. Wright of Rockbridge County, son of 1877 James Wright of August County

100.

1849 LAND TAX LIST

ROCKBRIDGE COUNTY, VIRGINIA

Appendix: Rockbridge County, Virginia, 1849 Land Tax List:

Robert S. Campbell District:

Name of Owner	Residence	Estate, whether held in fee simple, for life, &c	No. of Acres	Description of the land, as to watercourses, mountains and continguous tracts	Distance and bearing from the court-house	Value of land per acre, including buildings	Sum added to the land on account of buildings	Total value of the land and buildings

No Wrights listed

Appendix: Rockbridge County, Virginia, 1849 Land Tax List:

Robert S. Campbell District:

Name of Owner [continued from prior page]	Am't of tax on the whole tract, at the legal rate	Explanation of alterations during the preceding year, especially from whom transferred	Identification

No Wrights listed

Appendix: Rockbridge County, Virginia, 1849 Land Tax List:

Samuel Gold District:

Name of Owner	Residence	Estate, whether held in fee simple, for life, &c	No. of Acres	Description of the land, as to watercourses, mountains and contiguous tracts	Distance and bearing from the courthouse	Value of land per acre, including buildings	Sum added to the land on account of buildings	Total value of the land and buildings
Thompson A. Wright			58.120	Martha Johston hr	7 N	3.50		205.62
"			100	His own land	18 NE	4.00	25.00	400.00
"			200	Emanuel Reid	15	7.00	150.00	1400.00
"			54	Jas. Hull & his own	16	12.50	50.00	135.00
John Wright	Unknown		16.40	Jno. M. Bell on Nobb B.C. R	18 N	.12		32.50

Appendix: Rockbridge County, Virginia, 1849 Land Tax List:

Samuel Gold District:

Name of Owner [continued from prior page]	Am't of tax on the whole tract, at the legal rate	Explanation of alterations during the preceding year, especially from whom transferred	Identification
Thompson A Wright	.20		1854 Thompson A. Wright of Rockbridge County, son of 1815 John Wright of Prince William County, grandson of William Wright, great grandson of 1765 Richard Wright of Prince William County, and possibly great great grandson of 1700 Richard Wright of Stafford County
"	.40		
"	1.40	Wm Norcross	
"	.13		
John Wright	.03	Jos Bell	1836 John Wright of Rockbridge County

Appendix: Rockbridge County, Virginia, 1849 Land Tax List:

List C:

Name of Owner	Residence	Estate	No. of lots	Name of Town	value of Buildings	value of Lots Including Buildings	yearly rent @ $2.50	Amt of tax
Robt Wright	Rockbridge				60.00	75.00	15.00	.36
William G Wright				Brownsburg	100.00	150.00	30.00	.72

Appendix: Rockbridge County, Virginia, 1849 Land Tax List:

List C:

Name of Owner [continued from prior page]	Identification
Robt Wright	1847 Robert Wright of Rockbridge County
William G Wright	1904 William G. Wright of Rockbridge County, son of 1877 James Wright of August County

1850 LAND TAX LIST

ROCKBRIDGE COUNTY, VIRGINIA

Appendix: Rockbridge County, Virginia, 1850 Land Tax List:

<u>Samuel Gold District</u>:

Name of Owner	Residence	Estate, whether held in fee simple, for life, &c	No. of Acres	Description of the land, as to watercourses, mountains and continguous tracts	Distance and bearing from the court-house	Value of land per acre, including buildings	Sum added to the land on account of buildings	Total value of the land and buildings
John T Wright			2.00	Nathan Leakg Mill Cr	8 N.E	160.00	300.00	320.00
			.80	his Own land		8.50		4.25
John Wright	Unkn		16.40	Jos M Bell on Nobb BCPR	18 N	.12		32.50

2631(070609)

Appendix: Rockbridge County, Virginia, 1850 Land Tax List:

Samuel Gold District:

Name of Owner [continued from prior page]	Am't of tax on the whole tract, at the legal rate	Explanation of alterations during the preceding year, especially from whom transferred	Identification
John T Wright	.32	Tr fr M Lain 1849	
	.01	Tr fr Same 1850	
John Wright	.03	Jos Bell	1836 John Wright of Rockbridge County

Appendix: Rockbridge County, Virginia, 1850 Land Tax List:

Robert S. Campbell District:

Name of Owner	Residence	Estate, whether held in fee simple, for life, &c	No. of Acres	Description of the land, as to watercourses, mountains and continuous tracts	Distance and bearing from the court-house	Value of land per acre, including buildings	Sum added to the land on account of buildings	Total value of the land and buildings
Richard J Wright	Rockbridge	FS	285.110	Jas Riv S Brawford	16 S	10.00	250.00	2850.00

Appendix: Rockbridge County, Virginia, 1850 Land Tax List:

Robert S. Campbell District:

Name of Owner [continued from prior page]	Am't of tax on the whole tract, at the legal rate	Explanation of alterations during the preceding year, especially from whom transferred	Identification
Richard J Wright	2.85	From John Crawford 1850	1858 Richard Jordan Wright of Rockbridge County, son of 1804 Jordan Wright of Amherst County and grandson of Parmenos Wright

Appendix: Rockbridge County, Virginia, 1850 Land Tax List:

List C:

Name of Owner	Residence	Estate, whether held in fee simple, for life, &c	Number of each lot in the Town	Name of Town	Value of buildings	Value of lots, including buildings	Yearly rent of lots	Amount of tax on lots at the legal rate
Robt Wright	Rockbridge				60.00	75.00	15.00	.36
Wm G Wright				Brownsburg	100.00	150.00	30.00	.72

Appendix: Rockbridge County, Virginia, 1850 Land Tax List:

List C:

Name of Owner [continued from prior page]	Explanation of alterations during the preceding year	Identification
Robt Wright		1847 Robert Wright of Rockbridge County
Wm G Wright		1904 William G. Wright of Rockbridge County, son of 1877 James Wright of August County

INDEX

Bell, J, 51
Bell, Jno., 72
Bell, Jno. M., 64, 80, 88, 96, 104
Bell, Jos:, 15, 19, 33, 39, 46, 51, 52, 60, 65, 73, 81, 89, 97, 105, 111
Bell, Jos M, 110
Bell, Jos., 29
Bell, Joseph, 24, 56, 57, 60, 61
Crawford, John, 113
Elliot, Jas., 16, 80, 88, 96, 104
Johnston, Martha, 51, 56, 60, 64, 72, 80, 88, 96, 104
Lain, M, 111
Logan, Thos, 4
McKinsey, Jno, 73
McKinzie, J, 60
McKinzie, Jno, 64
Mill, Nathan Leakg, 110
Norcross, Wm, 64, 65, 105, 81, 89, 97
Reid, Emaniel, 80, 88, 96, 104
Reid, Maniel, 72
Reid, Manuel, 60, 64
Renney, W, 61
Simpson, Tho., 10
West, Jas, 46
Wiseman, G, 61
Wright, Charles, 4
Wright, John, 15, 16, 19, 20, 24, 25, 29, 30, 33, 34, 39, 40, 46, 51, 52, 56, 57, 60, 61, 64, 65, 72, 73, 80, 81, 88, 89, 96, 97, 104, 105, 110, 111
Wright, John T, 110, 111
Wright, Richard J, 112, 113
Wright, Robert, 9, 10, 35, 41, 47, 48, 53, 58, 62, 68 74, 75, 82, 83, 90, 91, 98, 99, 106, 107, 114, 115
Wright, Thompson A., 46, 51, 52, 56, 57, 60, 61, 64, 65, 72, 73, 80, 81, 88, 89, 96, 97, 104, 105
Wright, William G, 58, 62, 68, 74, 75, 82, 83, 90, 91, 98, 99, 106, 107
Wright, Wm G, 114, 115

Other Heritage Books by Robert N. Grant

Identifying the Wrights in the Goochland County, Virginia Tithe Lists, 1732-84

The Identification of 1809 William Wright of Franklin County, Virginia, as the Son of 1792 John Wright of Fauquier County, Virginia, and Elizabeth (Bronaugh) (Darnall) Wright

Wright Family Birth Records (1853-1896) and Marriage Records (1788-1915): Franklin County, Virginia, 1853-1896

Wright Family Birth Records, 1853-1896; Marriage Records, 1761-1900; Census Records, 1810-1900, in Amherst County, Virginia

Wright Family Birth Records, 1853-1896; Marriage Records, 1808-1910; Census Records, 1810-1900; Patent Deeds and Land Grants; Deed Records, 1808-1910; Death Records, 1853-1896; Probate Records, 1808-1900, in Nelson County, Virginia

Wright Family Birth Records, 1853–1896; Marriage Records, 1777–1918; Census Records, 1810–1900; Deed Records, 1777–1902; Death Records, 1853–1896; Cemetery Records, and Probate Records, 1777–1909; in Rockbridge County, Virginia

Wright Family Birth Records (1853-1896) and Marriage Records (1782-1900): Campbell County, Virginia

Wright Family Birth Records, Marriage Records, and Personal Property Tax Lists: Appomattox County, Virginia

Wright Family Census Records, Deed Records, Land Tax Lists, Death Records and Probate Records: Appomattox County, Virginia

Wright Family Census Records: Bedford County, Virginia, 1810-1900

Wright Family Census Records: Campbell County, Virginia, 1810-1900

Wright Family Census Records: Franklin County, Virginia, 1810-1900

Wright Family Death Records (1853-1920), Cemetery Records by Cemetery, and Probate Records (1782-1900): Campbell County, Virginia

Wright Family Death Records (1854-1920), Cemetery Records by Cemetery, and Probate Records (1785-1928): Franklin County, Virginia

Wright Family Death, Cemetery and Probate Records: Bedford County, Virginia

Wright Family Deed Records (1782-1900) and Land Tax List (1782-1850): Campbell County, Virginia

Wright Family Land Grants (1785-1900) and Deed Records (1785-1897): Franklin County, Virginia

Wright Family Land Grants, Deed Records, Land Tax List, Death Records, Probate Records: Prince Edward County, Virginia

Wright Family Land Records: Bedford County, Virginia

Wright Family Land Tax Lists: Franklin County, Virginia, 1786-1860

Wright Family Land Tax Lists: Rockbridge County, Virginia, 1782-1850

Wright Family Land Tax Records: Amherst County, Virginia, 1782-1850

Wright Family Land Tax Records: Nelson County, Virginia, 1809-1850

Wright Family Patent Deeds and Land Grants, 1761-1900, Deed Records, 1761-1903; Chancery Court Files, 1804-1900; Death Records, 1853-1920; Cemetery Records by Cemetery; and Probate Records, 1761-1900, in Amherst County, Virginia

Wright Family Personal Property Tax Lists: Amherst County, Virginia, 1782-1850

Wright Family Personal Property Tax Lists: Campbell County, Virginia, 1785-1850

Wright Family Personal Property Tax Lists: Franklin County, Virginia, 1786-1850

Wright Family Personal Property Tax Lists: Nelson County, Virginia, 1809-1850

Wright Family Personal Property Tax Lists: Rockbridge County, Virginia, 1782-1850

Wright Family Personal Property Tax Records for Bedford County, Virginia, 1782 to 1850

Wright Family Records: Births in Bedford County, Virginia

Wright Family Records: Land Tax List, Bedford County, Virginia, 1782-1850

Wright Family Records: Lynchburg, Virginia Birth Records (1853-1896), Marriage Records (1805-1900), Marriage Notices (1794-1880), Census Records (1900), Deed Records (1805-1900), Death Records (1853-1896), Probate Records (1805-1900)

Wright Family Records: Marriages in Bedford County, Virginia

Wright Family Records: Prince Edward County, Virginia Birth Records, Marriage Records, Election Polls, and Tithe List, Personal Property Tax List, Census